teacher's friend publications

Reproducible Pages for Early Learners!

Little Kids... Write!

Trace and Write Pages for Developing Beginning Writing Skills!

Written and Illustrated by:
Karen Sevaly
Contributing Editor:
Libby Perez
Graphic Designer:
Cory Jackson

**Look for All of Our
Little Kids... Books
at your local educational retailer!**

Table of Contents

Copyright © 2000
Teacher's Friend, a Scholastic Company.
All rights reserved.
Printed in China.

ISBN-13 978-0-439-54956-1
ISBN-10 0-439-54956-6

Safety Warning! The activities and patterns in this book are appropriate for children ages 3 to 6 years old. It is important that children only use materials and products labeled child-safe and non-toxic. Remember that young children should always be supervised by a competent adult and youngsters must never be allowed to put small objects or art materials in their mouths. Please consult the manufacturer's safety warnings on all materials and equipment used with young children.

Little Kids... Books!

Welcome to the wonderful world of young learners where play is learning and learning is fun!

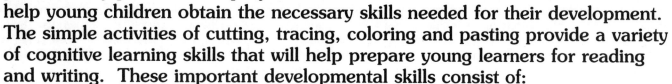

With these *Little Kids...Books!*, teachers can provide easy patterns and projects that will help young children obtain the necessary skills needed for their development. The simple activities of cutting, tracing, coloring and pasting provide a variety of cognitive learning skills that will help prepare young learners for reading and writing. These important developmental skills consist of:

Fine Motor Skills
> finger-wrist dexterity, arm-hand movement, eye-hand coordination

Perceptual Motor Skills
> identification, color and shape recognition, matching and location, spatial relationships

Expressive and Receptive Language Skills
> listening, speaking, questioning, relating words and pictures, imitation, utilization, recognition and discrimination, visual perception and discrimination

Social and Emotional Skills
> creativity and imagination, pride in accomplishments, self-reliance, self-control, self-confidence

The early years of schooling helps determine how a child will learn for a lifetime. During this period, children develop a sense of self and decide whether school is a burden or a joy. We hope these books assist you in your goal to provide each child with a fulfilling and fun learning experience!

Introduction

Little Kids...Write!

As small children develop their language skills and begin to relate to written language, teachers should introduce a wide variety of play-based activities associated with literacy. Activities such as singing songs, reading and telling stories, drawing pictures, tracing lines and shapes, and many more, all encourage young children to begin reading and writing. By giving young learners a variety of writing experiences, they will begin to understand the important concepts essential to their success in literacy, such as: knowledge of words and their function, that words read aloud are represented by words on a page, that text is read from top to bottom and from left to right and that words are separated by spaces, etc.

EMERGENT WRITING - Small children can begin writing before they can write letters. This form of writing, known as "emergent writing," is essential in providing fine motor, expressive and receptive language skills. Encourage children to write their own stories without the hindrance of conventional writing and spelling. At first, children will write using scribbled, letter-like forms and inventive spelling. Let the children know that it's okay to write in "kid" writing and that it doesn't need to look like "grown-up" writing. Encourage them to "read" their writing aloud when they are done. As the children begin to identify letters by their shapes and forms, encourage them to write the letters. Have them use the letters to begin writing words and sentences in their writing activities. Prior to writing the letters, children need practice in tracing lines, curves, circles and shapes. (We recommend Teacher's Friend Reproducible Book, TF1453 Little Kids Can...Trace!) Here are a few ideas to assist you in working with emergent writers:

- It is important that you model the proper way to write each letter. Do this several times before you have the child attempt to trace the letter. Show each of your strokes in the same way each time the letter is written.
- The tracing letters and numbers found in this book have arrows that show you how to correctly print. (Letters and numbers are represented in simple manuscript style.) Start at the number one arrow and make the stokes in order, tracing over the dotted lines.
- As the child gains confidence in their tracing abilities, have him or her try writing the individual letters without tracing. Make sure they continue to use the proper strokes in the correct order.
- Have the children use oversized pencils or pencils with "pencil grips." Provide plain paper when children are first learning to write their letters. (Young children often have difficulty staying within the lines of lined paper.) When they are ready for lined paper, use primary writing paper with lines no less than 1 inch (2.5cm) apart.
- Instruct each child to place the paper straight up-and-down on the desk or table top. (Slant the paper to the left only for teaching traditional cursive or modern manuscript.) Children should sit in a chair with a straight back and one of appropriate size.
- After each new letter has been introduced to the class, use a center activity to reinforce good handwriting skills. Stock a center with manuscript paper, pencils, crayons and construction paper sheets with the new letter written on them. Students can use a variety of crayons to trace the letter several times before practicing the letter on handwriting paper.

DICTATION PAGES - In this book, you will find several dictation pages that can be used for emergent writing exercises. Some of the dictation pages are divided into three sections. The top section is designed to be used by the child writing his or her story in "kid" writing. The teacher then copies the child's story in the center section using "grown-up" writing as the child reads the story aloud. (The child can also illustrate their story on a separate piece of paper that is attached to the dictation page.) As the child begins to write letters, urge him to rewrite the story in the third section with your model as their guide. In the beginning, there will still be a great deal of inventive spelling and letter reversals. Use this time to talk to the child about letters, words and sentences. Explain to him or her the difference between drawing and writing and how words are separated by a space. Assist the child in finding the letter of the day in their writing or the words they already know.

There are also dictation pages in this book for children to simply draw a picture at the top of the page. The teacher can then ask the child to tell about his picture in story form. The teacher then writes the child's story under the picture using proper form and punctuation. The child can then "read" their story to others.

Each child's dictation pages can be collected and bound into a book that will serve as a practical example of the child's progress. Pages can be laminated and placed in a binder or held together with rings. This provides a fun way in which the child can share his or her stories and pictures with others. You may want to video tape the children reading their emergent writing stories.

PHONEMIC AWARENESS - With writing letters comes letter sounds. During these early years, most children naturally acquire some ability to think about the sounds of letters and spoken words without necessarily being aware of their meaning. Your responsibility is to assist youngsters in understanding the principle that letters have sounds and that these sounds make words. It is important that you provide activities and experiences to teach phonemic awareness along with basic writing skills. It has been proved that children are better equipped to begin reading if they are aware of the phonemes in spoken words. You should motivate the children with a print-rich environment and have available to them materials and manipulatives to help them learn these essential concepts.

As children begin writing letters, numbers and simple words, make sure that the child is taught to form the letters in the same way they will later learn in school. The first word the child should be taught to write is his or her name. Make sure you teach the beginning letter in uppercase and the remaining letters in lower case. You also need to make sure that the child is ready to learn to write before beginning any instruction. A child's desire to write is one criteria in which to judge his or her readiness. It is also essential that the child has demonstrated sufficient eye, hand and arm control before he or she can manipulate pencil and paper.

Writing and Literacy Practice for Emergent Readers and Writers

WRITING CENTER - Provide a variety of paper, writing utensils, envelopes, mailing labels, stickers, stamps, tape, stapler, etc. in an appropriate area of the classroom. Encourage students to write letters and stories even if they only use "kid" writing. Letters will become more recognizable as they learn to form letters and develop phonological awareness.

SHOW AND TELL LETTERS - Have the children bring in their favorite letters for show-and-tell. The letters can be in a book, on a cereal box or greeting card, or even on a t-shirt. Encourage the children to talk about their selected letter and discuss what sound the letter makes and what it looks like.

LETTER OF THE DAY - (Begin by selecting the letters that start the children's names.) Display a large cut-out letter on the class board. Post pictures and words that start with that letter around the board. Ask the children to compare other letters they have learned with the letter of the day. Show the children how to trace the letter on the board before having them trace the letter on paper. Draw an extra large letter in chalk on the sidewalk outside and have the children walk along the letter's shape. Have the children chant the appropriate part of the poem found on page 9, as they march around the letter.

CLASSROOM READING - While reading story books to your class, help children notice how words work in print. Make sure you point out and read the title and author's name before beginning a story. Show the children how words are separated by spaces and that the end of a thought ends with a period or punctuation mark. Occasionally run your finger under the words so children can understand that words provide thoughts and that text is written and read from left to right. Point out the parts of a book, such as sentences, paragraphs and chapters. Help them to know that a story does not necessarily end at the end of a page. After reading the story, ask the children questions about the story.

PURPOSE OF PRINT - Demonstrate how print in books, magazines, newspapers, etc. gives us information. Show them how to look up the day's weather in the newspaper or locate a recipe in a cookbook. Talk to the children about notes or flyers being sent home to parents and how they provide information that their parent needs. Demonstrate how to make a list and encourage them to make their own lists using "kid writing." Point out street signs and advertisements and talk about the information they give us.

LIBRARY CENTER - Provide a comfortable well-lit corner of the classroom with soft chairs and pillows. Have available a wide assortment of picture books and emergent readers that the children can "read" for themselves. Encourage the children to "check-out" books to take home overnight to read with a parent. Let children bring favorite books to school and share them with the class.

ALPHABET ACTIVITIES - Preschoolers that can recognize and print some letters of the alphabet will be more successful when they enter kindergarten. With this in mind, provide a variety of visuals and manipulatives that will encourage their alphabet learning, such as letter cards, wall charts, alphabet blocks, board games, bulletin boards, etc.

Group

Writing Skills Check List!

Names										
Traces Numbers										
Traces Letters										
Writes First Name										
Writes Last Name										
Writes using "Kid Writing" to express ideas.										
Uses Inventive Spelling										
Writes Upper Case Letters										
Writes Lower Case Letters										
Writes Numbers 1-10										
Recognizes some words by sight										
Writes Letters When Dictated										
Is Aware of Sentence Structure and Punctuation										
Writes some Words.										
Can Copy Simple Sentences										

I can write my letters & numbers!

_____
Name

_____ _____
Teacher   Date

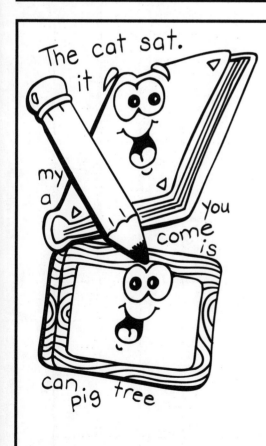

I can write words!

_____
Name

_____ _____
Teacher   Date

Manuscript Alphabet and Numbers

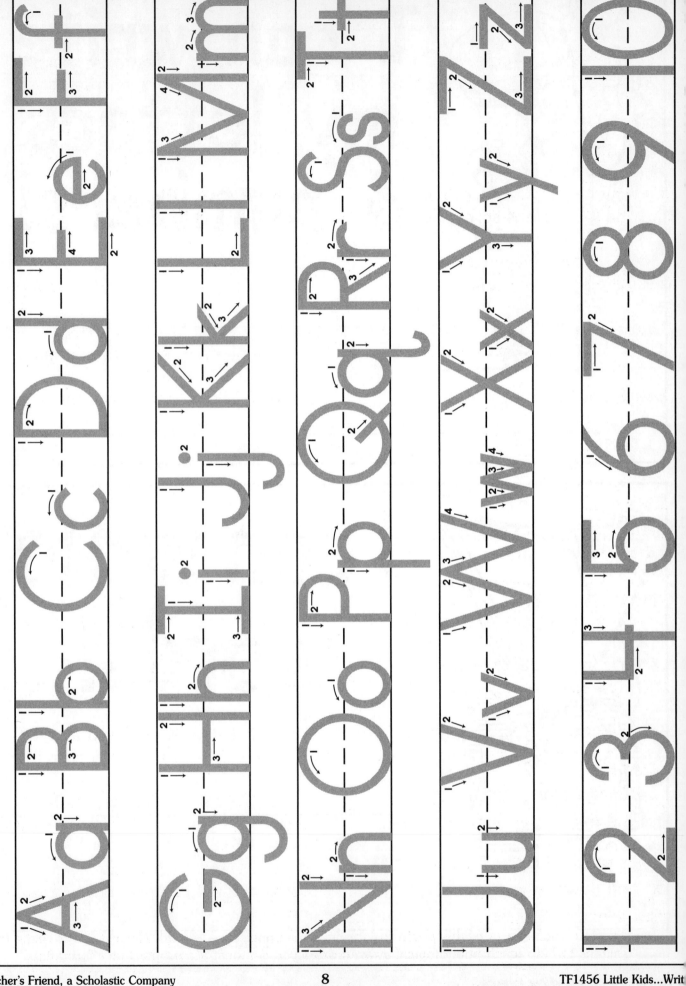

Alphabet Rhymes

Letter A says, "Apple, ant!"
Looks like a tent and that is that!

Letter B says, "Bear, bee, ball!"
It has two humps and that is all!

Letter C says, "Cat, cup, candy!"
Just half a circle is so handy!

Letter D says, "Day, dog, dish!"
Straight line, one hump, if you wish!

Letter E says, "Egg and eel!"
Three short lines is such a deal!

Letter F says, "Food, fish, fun!"
Looks like the E but minus one!

Letter G says, "Girl, go, gate!"
Add shelf to C, it looks just great!

Letter H says, "Hat, help, he!"
It has a bridge for you and me.

Letter I says, "Ice cream, ink!"
One line, two short, now give a wink!

Letter J says, "Jam, jump, jack!"
It's like a hook, so don't look back!

Letter K says, "Key, king, kite!"
Without a doubt, it's fun to write!

Letter L says, "Look, leaf, lie!"
Around the corner, just say "Hi!"

Letter M says, "Milk, me, mice!"
Up and down, it looks so nice!

Letter N says, "Nuts, nose, nest!"
Not quite a M, it's surely best!

Letter O says, "Octopus and old!"
Just like a circle, it looks so bold!

Letter P says, "Pig, pink, pan!"
Only half a B, if you can!

Letter Q says, "Queen, quilt, quit!"
Put a tail on O, now you've made it!

Letter R says, "Red, rug, ring!"
Short line on P is just the thing!

Letter S says, "Sock, sun, snake!"
Draw a snake and S you make!

Letter T says, "Time, top, two!"
One line with a hat, that's what you do!

Letter U says, "Up and under!"
Like a horseshoe, do you wonder?

Letter V says, "Van, vest, vine!"
Down then up, it looks so fine!

Letter W says, "Water, wind!"
An upside down M is now your friend!

Letter X says, "X ray" and that's it!
Two lines that cross, it's such a fit!

Letter Y says, "Yarn, yes, yup!"
You'll look like Y with both arms up!

Letter Z says, "Zebra, zoo!"
Zorro made it just for you!

Teacher: Use each stanza of this poem to introduce the upper case letters. Have students recite the rhymes to help teach phonological awareness as you demonstrate proper letter formation.

My Picture!

My Story!

My Picture and Story!

Dictation Page

TF1456 Little Kids...Write!

My Story

I can write my name!

I can write my name!

Trace and write these numbers.

1 | | | |

2 2 2 2

3 3 3 3

4 4 4 4

5 5 5 5

Trace and write these numbers.

6 6 6 6 — — — — —

7 7 7 7 7

8 8 8 8 8

9 9 9 9 9

10 10 10 10 10

Trace and write these letters. Color the pictures.

A A A A A A

B B B B B B

C C C C C C

Trace and write these letters. Color the pictures.

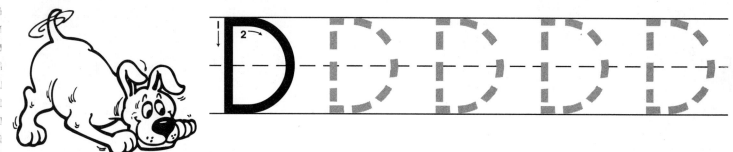

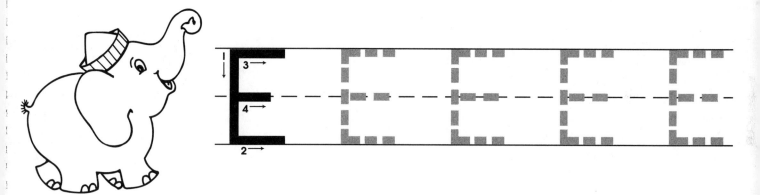

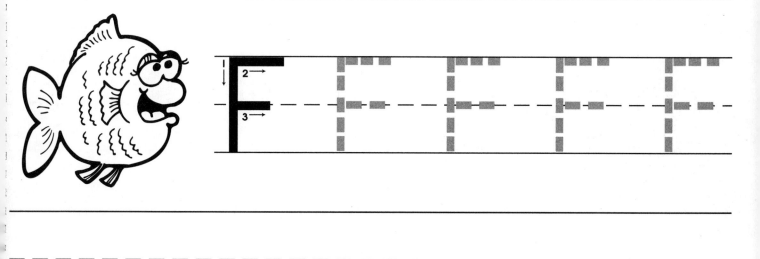

Trace and write these letters. Color the pictures.

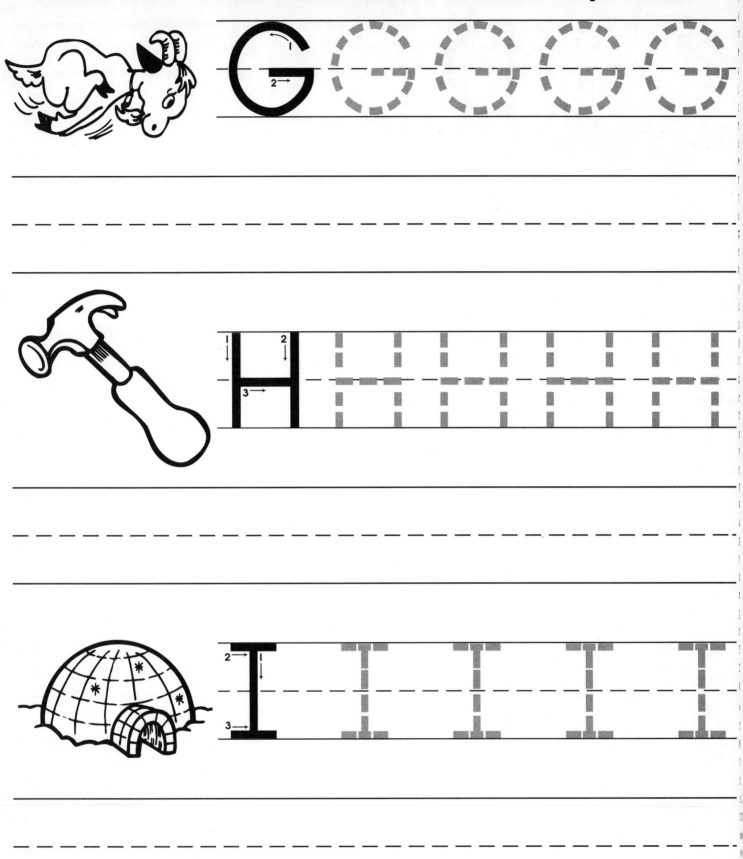

TF1456 Little Kids...Write!

Trace and write these letters. Color the pictures.

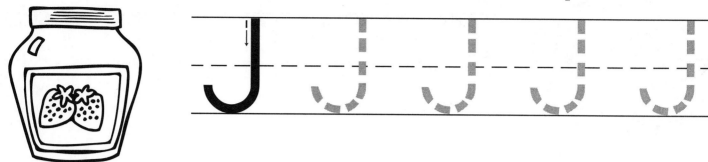

J J J J J J J

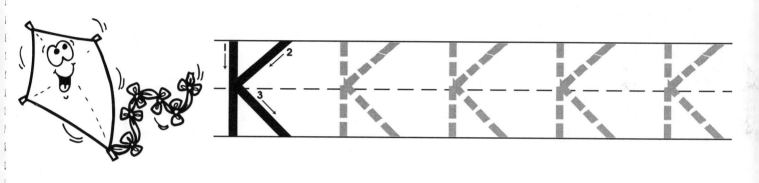

K K K K K

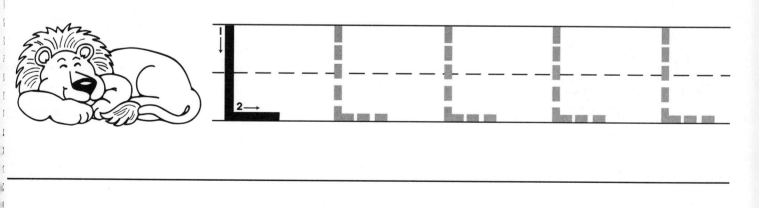

L L L L L

Trace and write these letters. Color the pictures.

M M M M M M M

N N N N N N N

O O O O O O O

TF1456 Little Kids...Write!

Trace and write these letters. Color the pictures.

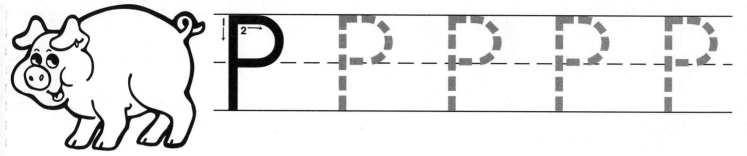

P P P P P P

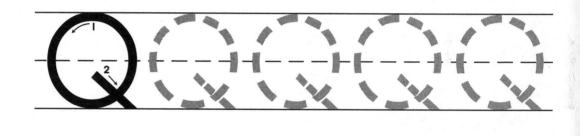

Q Q Q Q Q

R R R R R R

Trace and write these letters. Color the pictures.

S S S S S S

T T T T T

U U U U U U

TF1456 Little Kids...Write!

Trace and write these letters. Color the pictures.

V V V V V V V V V

W W W W W W W

X X X X X X

Trace and write these letters. Color the pictures.

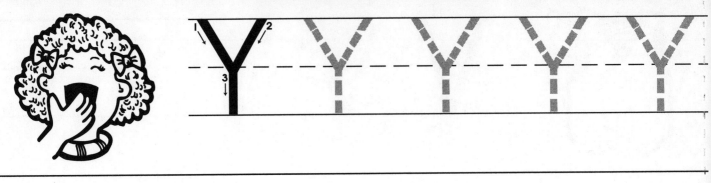

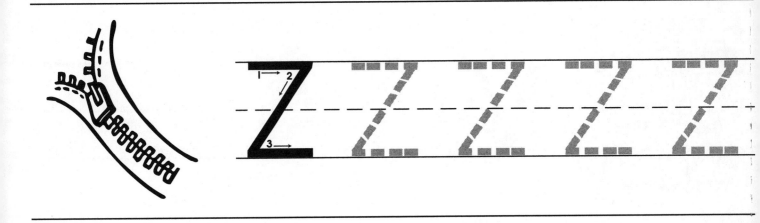

Trace and write these letters. Color the pictures.

a a a a a a

b b b b b b

c c c c c c

Trace and write these letters. Color the pictures.

d d d d d

e e e e e

f f f f f

28

Trace and write these letters. Color the pictures.

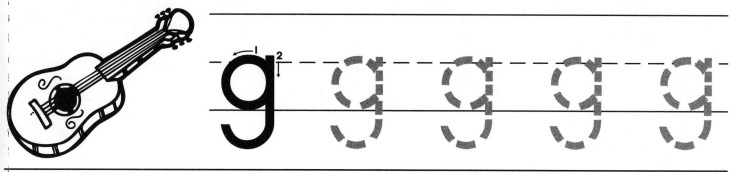

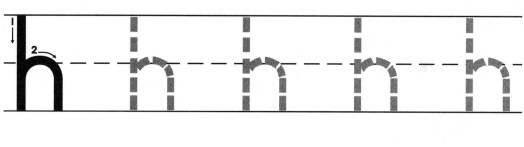

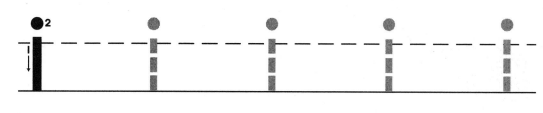

Trace and write these letters. Color the pictures.

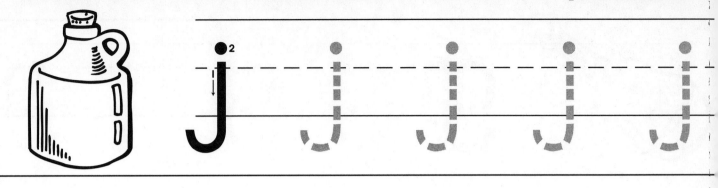

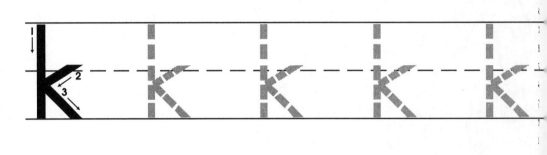

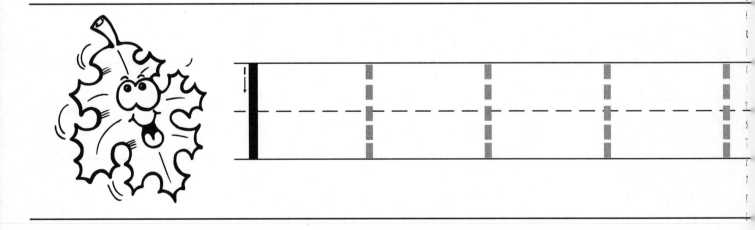

Trace and write these letters. Color the pictures.

m m m m m m

n n n n n n

o o o o o o

Trace and write these letters. Color the pictures.

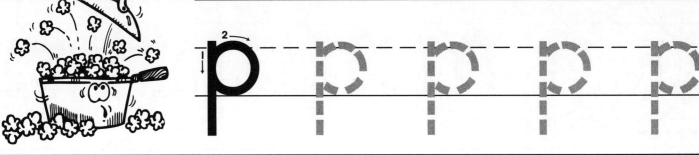

p p p p p p p p p p

q q q q q q q q q q

r r r r r r r r r r

32 TF1456 Little Kids...Write

Trace and write these letters. Color the pictures.

s s s s s s

t t t t t t

u u u u u u

Trace and write these letters. Color the pictures.

V V V V V V

W W W W W W

X X X X X X

Trace and write these letters. Color the pictures.

y y y y y y y y y y

z z z z z z

Trace and write these words. Color the pictures

ball

cat

sun

Trace and write these words. Color the pictures

bus

frog

cow

Trace and write these words. Color the pictures

fish

duck

pig

Trace and write these words. Color the pictures

dog

bee

hat

Trace and write these words. Color the pictures

tree

bird

bug

Trace and write these words. Color the pictures

star

girl

boy

Trace and write these high frequency "sight" words.

the

of

and

am

to

in

Trace and write these high frequency "sight" words.

is

you

that

it

he

was

Trace and write these high frequency "sight" words.

for

on

are

as

with

at

Trace and write these high frequency "sight" words.

be

this

have

from

or

had

Trace and write these high frequency "sight" words.

but

not

what

all

we

can

Trace and write these high frequency "sight" words.

an

she

do

how

if

will

Trace and write these high frequency "sight" words.

so

make

has

go

see

no